Affirming the Evangelist

Responses to *Good News People*

David Jeans

Principal of Wilson Carlile College of Evangelism

Daniel Cozens

Through Faith Missions

Ian Maher

Tutor and Lecturer, Wilson Carlile College of Evangelism

GROVE BOOKS LIMITED
RIDLEY HALL RD CAMBRIDGE CB3 9HU

Contents

The Cover Illustration is by Peter Ashton

Church Army and the Grove Evangelism Series

Church Army co-sponsors the publication of the Grove Evangelism Series as part of its aim of stimulating discussion about evangelism strategies, and sharing its experience of front-line evangelism. It has over 350 evangelists working in five areas of focus, at the cutting edge of evangelism in the UK.

Further details about Church Army are available from:
Church Army, Independents Road, Blackheath, London SE3 9LG.
Telephone: 0181 318 1226. Fax: 0181 318 5258.
Registered charity number: 226226

First Impression May 2000
ISSN 1367-0840
ISBN 1 85174 431 2

1
Introduction

Good News People is the report of a Church of England working party of the House of Bishops.[1] It looked at issues surrounding the growing number of local evangelists recognized by dioceses. It affirmed the importance and value of the distinctive ministry of the evangelist, and has been well received by the Church of England across the breadth of its traditions. It has undoubtedly raised the profile of evangelism and the evangelist within the Church of England—no mean achievement!

We have therefore found some tensions within ourselves as we have looked critically at the report. The criticisms which we do make are intended to be within a context of welcoming the report, and as a contribution to the on-going discussion of the distinctive ministry of the evangelist that the report itself recommends.

Inevitably, this discussion could be an 'in-house' Anglican matter. However, we hope that the issues raised will be of interest to evangelistic ministry in other denominations. And while familiarity with *Good News People* would obviously be helpful, this booklet can be read on its own.

We have also included some examples of the work of diocesan evangelists, all drawn from the diocese of Sheffield. We hope that these will help to earth the discussion.

Maureen works in an inner-city area of Sheffield. She does a lot of door-to-door visiting delivering a 12-page community handbook which includes community information plus a 3-page 'God-slot,' which includes explanation of some aspect of Christianity and some testimony. She comments on two developments for which this door-to-door work has shown a need—mid-week children's club, and ways to start dialogue between Moslems and Christians in the area. Maureen also regularly takes school assemblies and visits sheltered accommodation and a nursing home, sometimes to take services and sometimes to talk and pray with people.

---

1   *Good News People* (London: Church House Publishing, 1999).

2

Good News People and the Church of England

David Jeans

The Context of the Report

As the Church of England has prepared itself for the twenty-first century, it has experienced a welcome upsurge of interest in evangelism.

- Over three hundred delegates attended the Anglican Conference on Evangelism in March 1999.[2]
- In October 1999, the College of Evangelists was launched as a vehicle for recognizing the evangelistic ministries of those operating at a wider level than individual dioceses.
- Also in October 1999, the report *Good News People: Recognizing Diocesan Evangelists* was published.
- Both *Setting the Agenda* and *Good News People* were considered in the General Synod debate on evangelism on 16 November 1999.[3]
- Synod received *Good News People* warmly, commended it (and *Setting the Agenda*) to the dioceses for discussion and consideration, and strongly endorsed its first three recommendations.

Welcoming the Report

Such interest in evangelism is to be warmly welcomed by those with a concern for evangelism. *Good News People* has done a very good job in making the work of the evangelist 'respectable' in the Church of England. For example, it tries (pp 48ff) to counter some of the unfortunate caricatures attached to the word 'evangelist.' It affirms that:

- While evangelists are often challenging, they do not have to be difficult and uncooperative.
- Not all evangelists are evangelicals; in their researches on diocesan evangelists they found all traditions represented.
- Not all evangelists are preachers; communication of the gospel happens in a variety of ways, of which preaching is just one (albeit 'God-given').
- Evangelists are not itinerant loners; they found a great desire by evangelists to be rooted in and supported by a local church.
- Evangelists are seldom door-knockers and street-corner preachers; they work through a variety of methods, often relying on building up relationships.

2 See *Setting the Agenda* (London: Church House Publishing, 1999) for a report on the conference.
3 Reported in *Church Times*, 19 November 1999.

One of the great strengths of the report is its emphasis on the links between the evangelist and the church, both at local and at wider level. Its treatment of the mutual accountability between evangelist and local church is excellent. Ian Maher looks at this aspect of the report, along with issues of selection and training, in chapter five of this booklet.

The Place of Proclamation

The report reflects much recent thinking of the church in its emphasis on the importance of relationship, process and practical action.[4] While we would not want to deny the importance of any of these aspects of evangelism, we do wonder whether the report reflects a tendency in some parts of the church to downplay the role of proclamation.

There does seem to be some discord between the definitions of the work of the evangelist given on p 9 of the report and what is actually happening in the dioceses. The report itself points out that such definitions of the evangelist 'tended to emphasize the effective communication of the gospel as being central to the ministry of the evangelist.'

Yet the report's survey of diocesan practice concludes that 'the great majority of evangelists are not being used in "up-front" evangelism but in work within the parishes as visitors, nurture group leaders, etc' (p 20). One diocese is even described as having 'so great a desire to avoid the popular image of an evangelist that training in more up-front evangelism…was largely absent and some of the evangelists felt that they were ill-equipped for this role' (p 18). The issue of the report's view of evangelism and the ministry of the evangelist is explored further in chapter three.

Acceptability or Domestication?

A second major reservation stems from the report's understandable and welcome attempts to make the ministry of the evangelist more acceptable than it has sometimes been in the Church of England. Coupled with the otherwise excellent emphasis on the necessary links between the evangelist and the church, it runs the risk of domesticating the evangelist.

The Need for Pioneering

Similarly, the emphasis on evangelism rooted in the ministry of the local church is a necessary corrective to some views of evangelism. However, the context of postmodern (and arguably post-Christendom) Britain surely requires more radical and pioneering approaches to evangelism than envisaged by the report. Daniel Cozens looks at the issue of the need for pioneering in chapter four of this booklet.

---

4   See, for example, *Setting the Agenda* Section 1, and John Finney, *Finding Faith Today* (Swindon: Bible Society, 1992).

Church of England Evangelists—The Need for Clarity and Coherence

Good News People, because of the nature of its brief, concentrates on the ministry of local evangelists recognized by dioceses. Its examination of the present position is largely descriptive rather than prescriptive, except in its advocacy of proper selection, training and mutual accountability. This raises two issues:

- How do the understandings of the ministry of the evangelist adopted by different dioceses relate to each other?
- How do the various forms of evangelistic ministry (such as the College of Evangelists, Church Army evangelists, the evangelistic ministry of clergy including bishops, and other evangelists such as those working with Walk of 1000 Men, CPAS and Springboard) relate to one another and to the task of every member of the church to witness to Christ in his or her setting?

The report sees itself as surveying the work of diocesan evangelists in the Church of England at such an early (it uses the word 'experimental') stage that it would be 'entirely wrong' to suggest any blueprint (p 63). It goes on to offer 'questions for further consideration' that dioceses should take into account in addressing their local situations.

The most fundamental of these questions is 'What definition of evangelist do you wish to work with?' The working party that produced the report has done some work on the ministry of the evangelist in the New Testament and in church history, and acknowledges that more work needs to be done in this area. But it then contents itself with simply describing the understandings that exist in the different dioceses surveyed.

Is this descriptive approach is good enough? Can there be any clarity on the various current forms of evangelistic ministry if there is no common understanding of evangelism and the ministry of the evangelist? Of course different contexts for evangelism will require different varieties of evangelist, and we must refrain from too tight definitions that will inhibit evangelism in some contexts. 'Evangelism belongs to and is the calling of the whole church' as one diocese says (p 13).

Yet can it be right for a diocese to be able to refuse to have people with the label 'evangelist,' when it is a New Testament word (p 44)? Can it be right for one diocese to see evangelism 'increasingly as spiritual direction' (p 17), or for another to view their evangelists as 'Outreach Coordinators' (p 16)? We would not dream of each diocese having their own definition of ordination; even in the more controversial area of Ordained Local Ministry there are some starting points commonly agreed.[5] Should there not at least be an acceptable range of understandings of the ministry of the evangelist recommended to dioceses?

---

5   See *Stranger in the Wings* (London: Church House Publishing, 1998).

The report does acknowledge the need for more work to be done on the ministry of the evangelist and embodies this in its recommendation 7.2. A way forward might be an investigation of various approaches to evangelism through looking at other sources besides the work of existing diocesan evangelists. This might result in a greater variety of approaches in the dioceses such as mission-focussed, network-based and other pioneering models which could complement the low-key, relational and conventional church-based approaches described in the report. This is *not* a plea for tight definitions—rather it is hoping for an approach that will open the eyes of dioceses to a wider range of possibilities.

The Variety of Evangelistic Ministry

1999 saw an upsurge of awareness of a number of different evangelistic ministries. While consideration of the relationship between these different ministries was outside the brief of the working party that produced *Good News People*, it is clear that this is an area in which work urgently needs to be done. The range of evangelistic ministry in the Church of England covers the following (with apologies for any unintentional omissions):

- The daily witness of the people of God both in individual and communal life. This is fundamental to the spread of the gospel, and the exercise of specialist evangelistic ministry must not be allowed to minimize its importance.
- The ministry of the diocesan bishop, whose consecration services include references to the gospel and to mission.[6] In this context, it is interesting that General Synod's response to its debate on evangelism included an amendment calling upon 'every bishop, diocese and congregation to see that their primary task is to share in and show the love of God in Jesus Christ' and to continue the work of evangelism beyond the Decade.[7]
- The evangelistic ministry of the parish clergy, with their contacts with those on the edge of the church and outside the church. *Good News People* recognizes that some clergy are particularly gifted in evangelism, and recommends (7.5) that this should be recognized. David Sanderson, on the other hand, argues that the pressures on clergy in a normal parish role are such that it is not possible for them to fulfil the role of evangelist.[8]
- The ministry of diocesan lay evangelists, as discussed in *Good News People*.
- The ministry of those involved in missions and other special evangelistic events. This includes those involved at a 'professional' level such as diocesan missioners, Springboard, Church Army and CPAS evangelists, the leaders of Walk of 1000 Men missions. It also includes many lay people who have been trained in evangelism for and by such events.

---

6 See David Sanderson, *The Office and Work of an Evangelist* (Grove Evangelism Series Ev31) p 12.
7 See *Church Times*, 19 November 1999, p 5.
8 David Sanderson, *op cit*, p 15.

- The ministry of specialist diocesan missioners and advisers in evangelism, who may function as practitioners in evangelism or as reflectors on and enablers of evangelism—or both.
- The ministry of Church Army evangelists, who are admitted to the Office of Evangelist by the Archbishop(s) and commissioned by Church Army. They mostly operate in local settings, but are usually stipendiary. Increasingly, they are specializing in five areas of work (Area Evangelism, Church Planting, Children and Young People, Homeless People and Older People). Church Army has a broad understanding of evangelism, describing its work as 'sharing faith through words and action.' Church Army's vision includes a commitment to enabling and training others, and to pioneering and creative risk-taking in evangelism.
- The ministry of the members of the College of Evangelists, who will probably already belong to one of the above groups, but whose ministry is recognized as having a regional or national dimension.

The above represents a wide range of ministry. Some are clergy, some are lay, some are non-stipendiary, and some are stipendiary. Also within the lay evangelists, some have no recognition (those who take part in missions, for example), some have limited local recognition (diocesan evangelists), and some have national recognition (Church Army evangelists and lay members of the College of Evangelists).

Responses to the Variety of Evangelistic Ministry

There are various reactions to such a bewildering variety. One reaction is to be excited by the very existence of so many different ways of expressing the Great Commission! The Bishop of Southampton expressed this view well in a letter to *Church Times* (29 October 1999): 'The key thing is that our nation needs re-evangelizing, and there are very many different and complementary ways of doing it—even in the Church of England. This is not confusing, nor contradiction, but part of how the Spirit is responding to the multifarious needs of our time.' A more negative reaction has been that of frustration at the church 'reinventing the wheel' when it already has evangelists (Church Army), and has had them for over a hundred years![9] The report is, in fact, very positive about the role of Church Army, and recommendation 7.3 (which was passed by General Synod) urges the Church of England to support and make use of the experience and resources that it can offer.

A response somewhere between the two seems to be the most sensible. A variety of types of evangelist does seem to be necessary in the context of the year 2000 and beyond. Parishes need to be recognizing local evangelists, and

---

9   See the letters page of *Church Times*, 22 October 1999, and the Church Army Chief Secretary's reply welcoming both Diocesan Evangelists and the College of Evangelists in *Church Times*, 29 October 1999.

recommendation 7.7, which encourages the involvement of evangelists in setting up patterns of collaborative ministry, is to be warmly welcomed. Church Army and other recognized evangelists have a crucial role to play in the training and encouragement of such local evangelists.

However, such local church-based voluntary evangelists may have limitations in reaching 'beyond the fringe' of the local church. In post-Christendom England, does not the church need to be setting aside specialist evangelists to pioneer ways of reaching those parts of the nation that the local church is not reaching? This is surely an important future role for Church Army and other specialist evangelists, and is a distinctive task from that of the parochial ministry.

While the positive response to variety exemplified by the Bishop's letter above is to be welcomed, the real experience of many evangelists is that they often feel under-valued and sometimes marginalized.[10] This is one of the chief reasons why the issues of recognition of evangelists and the relationship between the different varieties does still need to be explored and clarified. The second task of the Working Party (*Good News People*, p viii) 'to examine the issues regarding office, order and recognition in relation to evangelists' remains incomplete.

Conclusions

Good News People has affirmed the value of the distinctive ministry of the evangelist, and has resulted in the dioceses being obliged to consider such ministry. It is to be hoped that this will result in the growth of such ministry, a development to be welcomed provided that it is not at the expense of domesticating evangelistic ministry within the church.

Christine comes from a steel-making community between Sheffield and Rotherham. She is 'embarrassed' at how much she does in the community compared with in the church. Her full-time employment is as a labour market worker with the local forum, but she is also a member of a safety group, treasurer of the local advice service, and on the committee which makes decisions on local bids for Single Regeneration Budget funding.

In the church she is an encourager in evangelism. In the year 2000 she has been involved in a project to deliver a *Jesus* video to every home in the parish, and in encouraging the church's cell groups to take part in the Luis Palau mission held in April in Sheffield.

---

10   The failure of any of the main speakers at the Anglican Conference on Evangelism to even mention the work of Church Army evangelists being a case in point.

3

What is an Evangelist?

David Jeans

Good News People pleads for the importance of the word 'evangelist.' It argues that 'it is a New Testament word, which needs to be rescued from caricature and honoured' (p 44). It also points out that 'its use seems to occur in times of considerable missionary expansion and to wither almost to nothing when either persecution or apathy curtails the expansion of the church.' Its rediscovery through the Decade of Evangelism and General Synod's acceptance of this report is highly significant for the mission of the church in twenty-first century England, when missionary expansion is certainly needed!

The report looks at the use of the word 'evangelist' in the New Testament and through church history, acknowledging that there had been very little previous work done for them to utilize in their investigations. They also made a decision to concentrate on the use of the word 'evangelist' rather than to look at the history of evangelism (p 26).

The Evangelist in the New Testament

The report's survey of the use of the word 'evangelist' in its three occurrences in the New Testament (Acts 21.8, Ephesians 4.11 and 2 Timothy 4.5) leads it to conclude that the work of the evangelist is both proclamation and service, and that it is directed towards those inside the church as well as those outside it. It also claims that The New Testament 'encourages us towards a holistic definition of the word.'[11]

The Evangelist and Proclamation

The report is very clear in some places on this issue. After discussion of the much more frequently used New Testament words *euangelizesthai* (to proclaim good news) and *euangelion* (good news) in sections 3.7 and 3.8, it concludes that 'the evangelist is the messenger who proclaims good news' (p 28) and that the work of the evangelist is the 'proclamation of the good news' (p 29). In this it clearly picks up the centrality of proclamation in the understanding of the word 'evangelist' and its cognates. However, it does seem to want to qualify this in some of its other conclusions.

The Evangelist and Service

The example of Philip is surely being stretched beyond its limits when the report describes him as both serving the Christian fellowship and proclaim-

---

[11] *Good News People* sections 3.13, 3.17, 3.27, 3.28.

ing the good news, and using this to incorporate both proclamation and practical service into the work of an evangelist (p 38). In Acts 21.8 Philip is described as an evangelist, and also as one of the seven 'deacons' from Acts 6. He thus could be seen as exercising two different forms of ministry at different stages of his life.

In Jerusalem, he is one of the deacons appointed to serve at tables. After the scattering of the church through the persecution that followed the stoning of Stephen (a persecution used by God to force the cosy Jerusalem church to obey the command of Acts 1.8 to go to Samaria and to the ends of the earth?), Philip is to be found proclaiming Christ in Samaria, and engaging in one-to-one evangelism with the Ethiopian eunuch. In his ministry as an evangelist he had moved away from his ministry serving at the tables. While it is hoped that he retained the heart of a servant, his ministry had changed so that by Acts 21 he is called 'Philip the evangelist' alongside his other recognition as one of the Seven. The two ministries are distinct.

The link between the evangelist and service in Ephesians 4 is a little forced, depending as it does on a disputed understanding of the Greek text. The report follows the interpretation of Andrew Lincoln[12] in seeing the work of service as belonging to the ministries of verse 11, rather than the interpretation of Markus Barth and others[13] which sees the work of the ministries as equipping the church for its work of service. The most that can be said is that the evangelist should see his or her ministry as an act of service.

The same must surely be said of Paul. In 2 Corinthians 4.5 he describes himself as both proclaiming Christ Jesus as Lord and being a servant of his readers. This insistence on servanthood must be about his motivation, not about the sort of work that he undertakes. He sees his evangelism, his proclamation of the good news, as an act of service, rather than as something drawing attention to himself.

The statement of Section 3.13 that 'the work of an evangelist is both proclamation and service' is both accurate and important if it is understood as describing the desired servant attitude of the evangelist. However, if it is taken as endorsing the interpretation that the work of the evangelist in the New Testament includes practical acts of service it is claiming too much. The practice of evangelism today does rightly include such acts, but it is reading current practice into the New Testament to see such a pattern there!

The Evangelist and Teaching

Here the report is on firmer ground. The work of both Philip and Timothy clearly included explanation as well as proclamation and the gospels themselves were written as teaching and encouragement for believers, but have

12   Andrew T Lincoln, *Ephesians* (Dallas: Word Books, 1990) pp 253ff.
13   Markus Barth, *Ephesians* (New York: Doubleday, 1974) pp 478ff, F F Bruce, *Colossians, Philemon and Ephesians* (Grand Rapids: Eerdmans, 1984) p 349.

been used throughout Christian history as tools for evangelism (Section 3.23). The statement in Section 3.22 that 'evangelism and teaching belong together' may be slightly overstating the case, however. After all, the ministries of evangelist and teacher are separated in Ephesians 4, and some commentators have seen in the order of the ministries some indication that the work of the teacher and the pastor follows that of the evangelist,[14] although it could be argued that they are reading modern understandings into the text.

The Evangelist and the Church

Clearly the report is correct in pointing out the role that Timothy had both inside and outside the church. It develops an interesting argument (pp 29–34), based particularly on the letter to the Ephesians and the proclamation of 'peace to those who were far off and peace to those who were near' (Ephesians 2.17). The good news of reconciliation between God and humankind also encompasses reconciliation between Jews and Gentiles in the community of Christ's body. The Report therefore warns us 'against too readily rebuilding in our proclamation a dividing wall between those who are far off and those who are near, and against too sharply separating the gospel for outsiders from the gospel for insiders' (p 33).

The relevance for evangelism in the twenty-first century post-Christian context of the New Testament's wrestling with relationships between Jewish (insider) and Gentile (outsider) believers warrants further exploration. It raises huge questions for those involved in more pioneering attempts to take the gospel outside the church. How can converts made through alternative forms of church be integrated into the Christian community, and to what extent should they be so integrated as an expression of the reconciling power of the gospel? To what extent should the 'insider' community be willing to change to accommodate the outsiders as its response to the message of the gospel?

These questions demonstrate that working both inside and outside the church has to be part of the role of the evangelist, but this has to be done while retaining the emphasis of a 'ministry that functions on the boundary' (p xii).

The Evangelist in Church History

The working party had little previous work to use in investigating the word 'evangelist' in Christian history. What references they did find indicate that for the most part evangelization (or evangelism) and the work of evangelists were seen as directed towards unevangelized areas and peoples rather than unevangelized individuals. Such examples could be regarded as the work of missionaries and apostles as much as the work of evangelists. It would have been helpful if the report had included more detail about the contemporary work of evangelists in the wider Anglican Communion—the reference to the missionary bishops of Nigeria in section 2.51 was particularly tantalizing.

---

14 See for example Bruce, *Colossians, Philemon and Ephesians*, p 347.

It was also disappointing that there was no discussion of the role of female evangelists as exemplified in the missionary work of the past,[15] or by their involvement in the work of Church Army from its beginnings.[16] Incidentally, it would be interesting to know how many of the diocesan evangelists are women; the report clearly envisages that as a possibility, but gives no statistics. Sheffield diocese lists 24 lay evangelists in its 2000 *Year Book*, of whom 17 are women, but it is not clear whether this proportion is typical.

Several of the stories of diocesan evangelists scattered throughout this booklet are those of women, to help to redress the balance!

Another area about which the report is silent is that of evangelists specializing in work with children and young people, a somewhat surprising omission in the light of the Anglican Conference on Evangelism's resolution that a fund should be set up specifically for evangelism among young people.[17] Dioceses authorize children's and youth workers as well as evangelists; it would be interesting to know the extent of overlap between the two.

The Evangelist Today
Defining 'Evangelist'

The definitions given by the various dioceses 'emphasize the effective communication of the gospel as being central to the ministry of the evangelist' (p 9). *Good News People* comes to its own definitions of an evangelist on p 49. Evangelists:

- go where the church is not;
- proclaim and live the gospel;
- interpret the church to the world and the world to the church;
- come from the centre of the church and are accountable to it as well as challenging it;
- encourage the whole church in its work of evangelism.

The work of diocesan evangelists in practice, as described in *Good News People*, seems to be more accurately described in some of these points than in others. The last two seem to be well covered. The local church base of the evangelists researched by the working party is very strong. The number described as 'mission enablers' or 'outreach coordinators' suggests that the encouraging of the church in its work of evangelism is also well established.

Response

There are questions to be asked, however, about the first three points. There is little evidence of pioneering ministry 'where the church is not.'[18] Similarly, it is difficult to see examples of the interpretation of church to world and world

15 See Rosie Nixson, *Liberating Women for the Gospel* (London: Hodder & Stoughton, 1998).
16 See Donald Lynch, *Chariots of the Gospel* (Worthing: H E Walter, 1982) p 34.
17 *Setting the Agenda*, p 94.
18 See the next chapter for further discussion of the pioneering aspect of evangelism.

to church. The described ministries of evangelists are much too church-based and (paradoxically) people-based to engage significantly with the dialogue between church and world.[19]

In terms of proclamation and living, the situation is too heavily weighted towards the 'incarnational' approach compared with the 'proclamation' approach. The report is rightly very strong on evangelists living out the faith that they proclaim, and its codes of conduct for evangelists and their supporting churches are excellent. We certainly do not want any repeats of the scandals surrounding some American tele-evangelists.

Nevertheless, there does appear to be a reluctance in some of the dioceses to engage with the task of proclamation that is at the heart of the New Testament word 'evangelist.' Of course proclamation can be through one-to-one relationship, and the evangelistic ministry of the many diocesan evangelists who are working in that way is not to be dismissed.

Equally, loving service can be part of proclamation,[20] both to those who receive such service and to those who observe it and share in giving it, as explored by Raymond Fung[21] and by Ann Morisy.[22] Yet proclamation is pivotal to the work of the evangelist, and this distinctiveness is in danger of being lost in the cause of rescuing the evangelist from caricature. The failure of one diocese (p 18) to provide training for evangelists in proclamation does seem to be extraordinary.

Conclusions
Good News People is very concerned to treat the work of the evangelist 'holistically.' This is a valid approach, and may be helpful to those parts of the church who have struggled with the caricature of the evangelist. However, in this process the New Testament emphasis on proclamation (with all the variety of methods that it can encompass) must not be lost.

Chris lives in a large village between Rotherham and Barnsley. Recently some young people from the council estate, fed up with just hanging about on street corners, formed an action group to make a useful contribution to the community. When the Parish Council asked for a representative from the church to join the committee overseeing the action group, Chris volunteered. He sees this work as 'showing that the church cares about the community' and as a 'bridge-building exercise.' Through his involvement he is building relationships and getting alongside local young people.

The parents on the estate have now formed a tenants and residents association, and Chris has contacts there too.

19 Although the examples from Sheffield in this booklet show good engagement with the world.
20 As in the Church Army slogan 'Sharing Faith Through Words and Action.'
21 Raymond Fung, *The Isaiah Vision* (Geneva: WCC Publications, 1992).
22 Ann Morisy, *Beyond the Good Samaritan* (London: Mowbray, 1997).

4
The Need for Pioneering
Daniel Cozens

What is an Evangelist?

I believe an evangelist is essentially someone called by God to preach the gospel. Above everything else, an evangelist is a preacher of God's good news, with a burden from God that wants to see people brought out of darkness into light, out of death into life, out of sin into forgiveness, and out of the world into the kingdom of heaven. An evangelist is sent as an ambassador to preach to those outside the kingdom of heaven and endeavours to bring them to be reconciled to God.

Pioneering

The concept of evangelist as pioneer is completely absent from the report itself and I believe the most urgent need we have at the moment is for the church to go into the world before we lose the latent support for Christanity in society that we currently enjoy.

A Preacher 'Out There'

Evangelists are pioneers in at least three particular ways. In the first place, they are preachers 'out there.' In the gospels we see Jesus going to where the people were. He *did* preach within buildings and he *did*, on occasions, preach within religious buildings. But if you were to take away from the gospels the times when he was 'out there' and only kept in the times when he preached within a religious building then you would take away the majority of the gospels themselves.

It is of the utmost importance that evangelists are people who pioneer to bring the gospel to those who have no knowledge of it. They are gifted and anointed to do this; it is a work of God from beginning to end. Evangelists try to emulate what Jesus did in going to people—either in crowds, in small groups, or as individuals—and bringing to them the message of why Jesus lived and died upon the cross and how it is that people can have peace with God. They are very clear about their message.

There is a lot of talk these days—as indeed there was in the *Good News People* report itself—about 'holistic' evangelism, although the authors of the publication do not seem entirely sure about what this means. Within the report, there was no clear call to actually *preach*, as it states in Acts 20.21. Nor was there mention of the need for a clear for turning to God in repentance and faith in our Lord Jesus. This is the message that evangelists seek to spread with the boldness that God gives them. In their prayers, they are praying that

God will open a door for the word and they go to where the people are. If they preach within a building, they bless the building, so that God's peace will come upon it. They then, in what is hopefully an effective, gentle, but clear way, declare to the people the love of God—that they may see him, believe in him, respond to him and bear fruits that befit repentance.

A Loner Committed to the Church

Though pioneers, evangelists are essentially committed to the church and it is important, as the report stressed, that they should be members of the church and that they should be surrounded by people that care for both them and their families, to make sure that their 'shelf life' is the very best that it can be.

Despite being committed to the church and the body of Christ, they are in many respects loners. Their inspiration comes essentially from God, by spending time alone with him, seeking his ideas, his text and his gospel. They are often people who 'go alone' with the Lord and experience, as the apostle Paul did, that the Lord 'stands by and gives me strength.' They seek to be people who declare the good news of Jesus Christ to others without faith, whether the church joins them in that activity or not. But because Christian people bring their non-Christian friends to hear them, evangelists often find themselves preaching to the converted and so more often seek venues outside the church. Evangelists are essentially, therefore, preachers who pioneer.

Pioneering Initiatives

Secondly, evangelists are pioneers through the initiatives they create. We see that the apostle Paul took the initiative when he went to Athens, in that he adapted his message for the Greeks to a format with which they were able to identify. Today's evangelist must also seek to be adaptable.

The apostle Peter, when he went on a roof-top to pray in Acts 9, received a vision from God and was subsequently given the initiative to go where no man had ever been—to preach the gospel to those called Gentiles. We see back in history that the gospel was brought to our own country by Augustine of Canterbury and, in the same way, the gospel has now gone to almost every nation on earth. In addition, we see that there was a missionary enterprise within England in the 1870s and 1880s that was second only to the New Testament.[23] As such, creating initiatives is something that defines evangelists, either by finding themselves burdened with a problem which they feel they should resolve or by receiving a direct command from God to go and do such a thing.

It sometimes seems extraordinary that God chooses evangelists who may not be considered the ideal person for certain tasks. Look at John Wesley, an aristocrat sent to minister to the miners of Cornwall, or Hudson Taylor, a weak

---

23 Evidenced by the large number of centenaries of mission agencies celebrated in the 1970s and 1980s.

and poor man used mightily by God in winning the Chinese by taking the initiative to dress as they dress and to preach the gospel in their own language and in a way that was acceptable to their culture.

Contemporary evangelists have also sought to be adaptable. The Alpha course uses more modern methods of telecommunication and videos. In the Walk of 1000 Men we have sought to recreate the commission of the seventy (Luke 10) by going without money, sleeping on hall floors and preaching the gospel to the people that we find. As a result of this, thousands of people have come to a living faith in Jesus Christ. On average on each walk we receive invitations from some 450 churches and visit some 750 public houses. We normally take 2 years to prepare with the local churches before each walk and the local churches then look after the converts and nurture them in their newfound faith. In the past decade, we have trained between 4,000 and 5,000 men and women (although mainly men) who have actually then gone out in this style to proclaim the good news, both one by one and in groups to those who are outside the church.

Unfortunately, in today's society, we have a much less healthy fringe around the church than we ever had and those within it appear more ignorant of the gospel than they were in previous generations. Today, there also seem to be far less evangelists and far less proclaiming of the gospel. In addition, there seems to be the mentality that it is the 'process' rather than the 'crisis,' whereas the Bible teaches that both are necessary. Today more than ever we do need great initiatives from God's people.

The Need for Ordained Evangelists

The report made some mention of this, but the evangelist needs to be brought into the ordained ministry as well as the lay ministry. Although within the Church of England's selection conferences we still emphasize the pastoral role of the nature of the Church of England, I do believe that there also remains a need to invite and ordain evangelists to work within the parishes. It has been my considered opinion over these past years that the organization I work with ('Through Faith Missions') could not have brought so many recruits to work with us had we not been an Anglican ministry with three ordained people leading it.

Evangelists therefore must be sought. They must be seen to be as important as the Bible makes them. They should be trained—by other evangelists, as well as theologians—so that their ministries may be as full as they can be and kept on a good strong wire as they go out into the world, that they may be able to return to the churches for their fellowship and nurture.

Creating Other People's Ministries

Finally, the evangelist is a pioneer in creating other people's ministries. It was during a conference in Amsterdam in 1983 that I was struck with one fact in particular. An Indian evangelist was speaking and said that, within the

Epistles of 1 and 2 Timothy, Paul makes 75 injunctions to Timothy to 'get his act together.'[24] The question was asked at that conference from the platform, 'what are you [other evangelists] doing about bringing other young men and women to follow in your steps to have their own ministries?' I believe that we should start, from when people first become converts, to look out for their abilities.

We should go into Bible Colleges and Theological Colleges and help the staff to assist their students in realizing their own ministries. Evangelists need to be trained by evangelists. It is a mistake only to teach them theology; that evangelism is often taught at the end of a term when students are tired shows that the need for evangelism and its preaching is not central in the curriculum of our theological colleges.

As such, the evangelist, according to Ephesians 4, should 'equip the saints for the work of ministry.' This can be difficult, in that the evangelist may not feel that she is much of a teacher to others, but there is no doubt of the evangelist's significant role in the forming of the ministry of others. Jesus said 'come, and I will make you fishers of men.' John Collins, the person who led David Watson to Christ, was particularly influential in my own personal development as an evangelist. I remember the early 1980s when I and other evangelists heard him speak of the 'singular concept' of the prayer of commitment to receive Christ and how to engage ourselves with those outside the church. The use of illustrations, the use of commentaries, how we would handle the different occasions of preaching in a cathedral or in an auditorium or at a dinner—these things need to be taught.

The report itself was cautious and kind, but the thing that it seemed to me most short of was any enthusiasm about the role of the evangelist. We need to search for and encourage those people with the gift of the evangelist to train them so that they are preaching the true gospel but also adaptable in their methods and able, in particular, to command the attention of the young.

Conclusions

Evangelists are pioneers. They preach to those outside; they create initiatives in following God's leading; and they help to develop the ministry of others. They spend time alone with God and the good news that they preach is seen within their own heart and life. They venture out from the shores of the church to 'launch into the deep,' where the real need is. They must be able to deal with mortifying disappointments, enormous criticism, but must, at the last, be resolved to preach the gospel of Christ 'out there.' The evangelist is one who goes after God, seeks his plans and then puts them into practice.

As Christians, we have a fight on our hands. In this generation, this battle is not against riches, or the media, or lack of enthusiasm but against fear. In whatever way we express it, we need to be teaching quite plainly that the

---

24 J D Douglas(ed), *The Work of an Evangelist* (Minnesota: World Wide Publications, 1984).

church is here to see men and women converted to Christ, built up in the holy faith, cared for, loved, realizing the wholeness that Christ gives, and encouraged to go into the world and tell the gospel to those outside. This is what Jesus says; it is outreach, not 'in-drag.'

Kate grew up and lives on a UPA estate in North Sheffield. She knows and is known by lots of people on the estate, and this gives her leadership of the church plant on the estate credibility. In the church plant she leads worship and preaches; she also takes school assemblies, and services in homes for the elderly.

Kate also has considerable community involvement. She is the area community representative on the committee looking at bids for Single Regeneration Budget funding, and is on the Management Committee for the estate's community centre which the church plant uses (and which the church helped to get built). She also finds time to sit on committees working on crime, health and social issues in the area. Somehow she has also nearly completed a Diploma in Evangelism Studies at Wilson Carlile College of Evangelism!

5
Selection, Training, Support and Accountability of Diocesan Evangelists
Ian Maher

This whole discussion is premised on the contention that while evangelism is a ministry of the whole church as the body of Christ, it is also a specific ministry for some people so called by God. There is an analogy here with the priesthood of all believers that encompasses all Christians and the specific call of some to the ordained ministry. In the Anglican context of *Good News People* this refers to the threefold order of bishop, priest and deacon.

God not only calls, but equips people with gifts necessary for evangelistic ministry. *Good News People* recognizes this fact and draws attention to the need for integrating evangelists into the life of the church. In so far as the profile of evangelism is raised through this process (*eg* through the recognition of evangelists in a diocese), it represents a positive step forward.

However, there is a tendency within *Good News People* to domesticate the ministry of the evangelist, locating it primarily within the orbit of the church community, limiting it within the traditional model of church at the centre of the community working out through concentric circles to touch the unchurched and de-churched. In a post-Christendom society it is increasingly evident that new models of being church are also needed. A considerable amount of literature has already been published to support this claim.[25]

While the importance of encouraging and enabling the church in its traditional parish expression to corporately witness to its faith should not be underestimated, it is surely a mistake to limit the exercise of the evangelist's ministry to this conventional but diminishing sphere of the church's influence. The danger is that the direct encounter of women and men specifically called and gifted by God to share the gospel with those who have never heard it will be minimal. The evangelist thus becomes part of the Christian 'ghetto.'

In whatever way it takes place, the common thread in evangelism is that people are brought into a face-to-face encounter with the challenge that Jesus Christ makes upon them. David Atkinson describes evangelism as 'that aspect of mission which consciously extends (by presence or proclamation) an invitation to those outside the faith to share in the life of the kingdom of God, and seeks for a response.'[26] Sensitivity and appropriateness are, of course, important but the sharp edge of the evangelist's ministry should not be underplayed and certainly not blunted. The old saying about the need for the church to 'comfort the disturbed and disturb the comfortable' is certainly true. Evangelists will, by the very nature of their call and the message they proclaim, be 'disturbers' as they seek to bring people into a life-changing encounter with Jesus Christ.

It is with the contention that the key distinguishing mark of the evangelist's ministry is the proclamation of the gospel—through words, actions or both—that the following responses to *Good News People* are made.

Selection of Diocesan Evangelists

Clear criteria are needed and a number of areas of consideration in selection are identified in *Good News People* at Section 5.3. For there to be agreement across the dioceses it is important that any such selection criteria are broad enough to encompass different approaches to, and styles of evangelism, various church traditions and diocesan distinctiveness. At the same time, the criteria need to be sharp enough to prevent the profile of evangelistic ministry from being blurred.

The Call and the Evidence

Alongside an enthusiasm for 'passing on the good news to others' (5.3.[a])—something probably held by far more people than are actually called by God

---

25 *eg Recovering the Past* by John Finney (DLT, 1996), *Building Missionary Congregations* by Robert Warren (Church House Publishing, 1995), and the ongoing *Encounters on the Edge* series of investigations by George Lings (The Sheffield Centre). See also *Hope From teh Margins*, Grove Evangelism booklet 49.
26 *God So Loved the World*, p 11, by David Atkinson (SPCK, 1999).

to be evangelists—there is a need to consider the evidence of a person's evangelist gifts. What examples are there to support a person in their call? In what ways has his/her ability to communicate the gospel been demonstrated in the context from which he/she comes? In other words, what fruit is there to show the authenticity of an evangelistic call? Have people come to a real faith, or developed a deeper faith in Christ through this person's ministry? Each of the definitions of evangelism cited in *Good News People* (p 9) incorporate this notion of tangible evidence of evangelistic gifts. The role of the local church community in which the candidate is located is clearly significant in the recognition of such gifts and any subsequent recommendation for training.

What Are We Looking For?

Some dioceses are aware of individuals already exercising an evangelistic ministry and are looking for appropriate ways of recognizing, utilizing and developing such gifts. Other dioceses are seeking to train 'potential evangelists' with 'possible rather than proven ability' but with a 'heart for evangelism' (2.3[d]). While the latter approach allows a wider net to be cast in identifying evangelists, there is a danger that the cutting edge of evangelistic ministry will be blunted by the recognition of people as evangelists who are not intrinsically evangelists. Having a 'heart for evangelism' is not necessarily the same as having the gifts of an evangelist. The danger can be averted provided there is a clarity about just what constitutes the ministry of an evangelist in practice. The ability to do the work of an evangelist is paramount. What makes the evangelist's ministry distinctive within the broader mission of the church is the ability as well as the enthusiasm to communicate the gospel.

Questioning the Assumptions

Good News People recognizes the importance of flexibility in the training of evangelists (5.1, 5.2), taking seriously the different starting points of people responding to a call from God. This is a positive acknowledgement of difference.However, there are some questionable assumptions about the sort of person that an evangelist should be. The requirement that an evangelist should be a person with 'a warm and relaxed personality allied to a sense of humour' (5.3[e]) suggests that evangelists must be cosy, cuddly people who never give offence.

While it is a good Christian witness to understand and respect others, affording them the dignity of people created in the image and likeness of God, the fundamental challenge of the gospel message to the values and standards of the world will at times make even the most relaxed evangelist a disturbing presence. It is unlikely that the apostle Paul would have made the *Good News People* grade as 'a warm, relaxed personality,' yet no one would question his evangelistic gifts.

21

A further point to consider in selecting evangelists relates to the breadth of evangelistic ministry. Some people have clear 'up front' gifts (*eg* evangelistic preaching, leading missions); others may be far more comfortable and effective in 'gossiping the gospel' in the context of their day-to-day encounters. There will also be those with a vision for communicating the gospel in new and novel ways out and beyond the present structures of the church. And there will be those who are motivators and enablers in evangelism, able to take people along with them in the evangelistic task.

Any selection process needs to be broad enough to encompass the different facets of evangelistic ministry, but sharp enough to distinguish the difference between the evangelist's ministry and that of, say, the ministry of a Pastoral Worker or Reader. In this respect the suggestions at 5.3 fall short and do not sufficiently address the distinctive nature of evangelistic ministry.

The Training of Diocesan Evangelists

Good News People rightly links the issue of training diocesan evangelists to the understanding of evangelistic ministry held within the diocese, and to the starting point of the candidates concerned. People will come from very different starting points and will benefit from a varied array of possibilities and options within the programme. Existing skills can be honed and new skills discovered and developed through a careful matching of needs with available resources (for example, modular components of Church Army's Certificate in Evangelism Studies). There is certainly no need for dioceses to expend unnecessary time and energy on developing training resources and materials when existing flexible material is at hand. This is a point well made by *Good News People* and supported with a useful list as one of its appendices.

Too Many Competencies?

The competencies list at 5.5 in *Good News People* is extensive to the point of being disabling. It may well, in its current form, be exclusive to many of the people that it seeks to attract. It is, arguably, over-prescriptive. While not underestimating the importance of a good balance in any training programme, it may be more realistic to operate with some broader categories of competency relative to evangelistic ministry. Within each category could be a range of sub-categories. Taking local ministry seriously, required competencies in the general categories could thus be met in a more tailor-made fashion and with far more relevance to the aspects of evangelistic ministry in the context within which the evangelist's call has been recognized. To illustrate the point, a person recognized as being someone with the ability to encourage others in evangelism might benefit from developing their adult education skills. For the gifted 'gossiper of the gospel' other skills will be more significant to develop.

The competencies list as it stands also makes assumptions about the academic level of women and men recommended for training as evangelists.

For some, it will be right and proper for their ministry to be grounded in the theoretical base presupposed by the list. It is also true that modern adult education approaches can (and should be!) making courses of high academic rigour accessible to many who were previously excluded by an educational elitism, including at the point of delivery.

Whilst all who are selected for training as evangelists should be encouraged and afforded the opportunities to stretch themselves, it may well be the case that a small but clear set of core competencies along with some specific training relevant to the local context of their ministry would be more appropriate than seeking to promote the broad sweep of the *Good News People* list for all local evangelists.

If the training of local evangelists is to take seriously the call of such people against the myriad of other demands upon their time, a careful balance will need to be struck between ensuring a well grounded, appropriate level of competency and over-stretching people with unrealistic expectations. Knowledge, formation and skills form a solid generic base for training. Core competencies across each that are relevant to all evangelistic ministry, along with a range of options reflecting its diversity might be a way of shaping the optimum level of training for diocesan evangelists.

Support and Accountability of Diocesan Evangelists

Good News People identifies well the importance of good support structures and lines of accountability (especially 6.2.3, 6.2.4, Appendices A and B). The evangelist's ministry will often take him/her beyond the 'comfort zone' of the church community. It is important that the local church understands this and does not place undue expectations for the evangelist to fulfil the role of other ministers (pastoral workers, Readers, curates).

The other side of the coin is that the evangelist needs to recognize his/her ministry as integrally bound up with the whole ministry of the local church and not independent of it, even though much time may be spent with unchurched people. *Good News People*'s Code of Conduct for Diocesan Evangelists and Code of Conduct for the Church in Relation to Evangelists provides an excellent framework for support and accountability.

The recognition of diocesan evangelists—the very subject that has generated *Good News People*—will itself be a considerable affirmation to those called by God to exercise an evangelistic ministry. It is a necessary precursor to the implementation of effective structures.

6
Conclusions
David Jeans

Good News People, in common with all reports (and these responses!) has its strengths and its weaknesses. It has affirmed the work of evangelists in a way that General Synod was able to approve, and that is no mean achievement. It has encouraged dioceses to think about having local evangelists and to take their training and care seriously. Its great strength is the essential link it makes between church and evangelist in terms of support, ownership and accountability. The codes of conduct are excellent models. Its insistence on the role of evangelist to encourage and stimulate the church, as well as to work outside it, should also be welcomed.

But its strengths also lead to its weaknesses. The model of evangelist that it has found in the dioceses is in many ways too easily accepted by the church. The downplaying of proclamation has the virtue of making the role of evangelist more accessible to the ordinary Christian, but it must not result in evangelists merely being another form of parish visitor, house group leader or practical carer. It is unavoidable that the evangelist uses some form of proclamation, however holistically that is understood. Similarly, the strong link to the local church should not result in domestication of the evangelist. There is an urgent need for more pioneering forms of evangelism, as Daniel Cozens has passionately argued.

The truth is that both ends of the spectrum need each other. *Good News People* represents an approach to evangelism that will work gently and quietly to bring God's love to people and situations. But the church's evangelism also needs the cutting edge represented by its pioneers and specialist full-time evangelists, particularly in today's context.

This again highlights the need to do further work on our understanding of evangelism. If all the varieties of evangelist are to complement and value each other, the issues of recognition, ownership and accountability must be addressed for the full-time specialist evangelists as thoroughly as *Good News People* has addressed them for the local, voluntary, diocesan evangelists.

Perhaps the most important lesson for the church, however, comes from the practical examples of the work of diocesan evangelists that have been given in this booklet. While the professionals discuss the right balance between proclamation, relationship and action, the diocesan evangelists whose work we have highlighted seem to have quite naturally found that balance in their ministries. It may be that it is their belonging to their local community that enables them to do this so well. Whatever the reason, we want to affirm them as evangelists and encourage others to follow their lead.